BARRY WATTS

More Amazing Magic

Illustrations:
MARK DAVID

Angus&Robertson
An imprint of HarperCollins*Publishers*

Introduction

Welcome to the Wonderful World of Magic! Soon you will be able to perform fascinating tricks that will amaze your parents, relatives and friends. Some of the most mysterious and magical tricks are very, very simple. Others require lots of study and practice.

Look through the book and find a trick that looks interesting. Study the instructions carefully and practice doing the trick by yourself several times to make sure you really understand how it works. Then go and try it on someone and watch their suprise!

Don't try to learn every trick at once. Select one at a time and learn each movement until you are able to present the trick naturally and confidently. That's the way to become a truly great magician. Even the tricks that look complex or difficult will eventually become easy to learn and perform if you simply spend some time practicing by yourself.

Most of the tricks in this book use everyday items like coins, handkerchiefs, glasses and cards. There are also some special ones you can make yourself.

Magicians have five big P's to guide them. If you follow the five big P's, you'll become a successful magician and be able to amuse and entertain audiences for many years to come. The five big P's stand for Professionalism, Practice, Patter, Preparation and Presentation.

'P' is for PROFESSIONALISM

You will learn many magician's secrets from this book. You will probably be surprised how simple some of them are.

Many magic tricks rely on very simple acts of misdirection — this means you will lead the audience to believe they are seeing you do one thing while you are actually doing something altogether different. Or you can make them expect one result while producing a different, surprising one.

It is very important that you do not share your professional secrets with anyone.

By keeping these secrets to yourself, you will be adding to the mystery and building your reputation as a person with very special skills, a really professional magician.

'P' is for PRACTICE

Practice is extremely important. It makes the difference between a performer who is poorly coordinated, drops things, and forgets the next step and

a magician who confidently entertains the audience with a dazzling array of magic skills.

Practice each trick until you find it easy to perform. If you can, practice in front of a mirror so you can see what your audience will see when you present the trick.

Keep practicing even when you feel confident about a trick. Study how to stand and where to hold your hands. Imagine how your audience is thinking. Have you told them enough about what you are doing?

The old saying 'Practice make perfect' certainly applies to 'student' magicians. Practice each step of your tricks, including how you move around the stage and what you have to say.

'P' is for PATTER

What you say while you are performing is called 'patter'. In many cases it is as important as the magic tricks themselves. So patter must be rehearsed, too.

Write down your patter for each trick. Suggestions about what to say are included with some of the tricks in this

book. As you practice a trick, say aloud the words that go with each step. Make sure you don't overlook any point.

Everything you say should help create an expectation in the audience about the trick you are performing. Sometimes you need to use patter to misdirect the audience, to lead them to expect one result while you know you will produce a different, surprising one. Patter can be very important in achieving this.

Remember, it is not necessary to explain everything. Just because you pick up an envelope doesn't mean you have to say, 'I am picking up this envelope.' You can remind the audience, though, that the envelope contains the prediction you made five minutes ago.

'P' is for PREPARATION

Every time you perform, check all your equipment (sometimes called 'props') well in advance. Make sure you haven't overlooked anything and see that each item to be used is absolutely ready to be picked up and presented.

Do you need to have pins, handkerchiefs, matches or rubber bands in your pocket? Have you put them in the correct pocket, ready to use?

Run through a list of the items you'll need to borrow from the audience to complete your tricks — have alternative ones close at hand in case you need them.

Do not rely on anyone else to bring a particular prop along, or to get it ready for you. You are the magician and must accept

responsibility for all aspects of the preparation as well as the performance.

If anything goes wrong during your performance, and sometimes it does, go back and start it again or press on with your next trick, rather than get flustered or embarrassed. Learn from the mistake. Why did it happen? How can you avoid it happening again? More rehearsal may be needed.

'P' is for PRESENTATION

As the magician, you are the center of attention. How you look, speak and move around the stage influences how the audience responds to your work.

Make sure your clothes or costume are clean and tidy.

Be happy and confident. Smile and talk clearly, and not too fast, to your audience. Look at their faces as you work — this helps them feel involved in your act.

Have all your magical equipment looking bright and colorful, too. Know where it is kept so you don't have to search for things during the show.

Practice how you move around the stage. Everything about your act should seem natural and unforced — no jerky movements or dashing around.

Remember that where you look and where you point will influence the audience to look in that direction, too. (Sometimes this is very helpful when you wish to misdirect the audience's attention.)

Use your face to express surprise, delight or worry in reaction to your tricks. The audience will respond in the same way. So don't look bored, or your audience may feel bored too.

Color Changing Wand

This simple trick is ideal for getting your audience's attention at the beginning of a performance.

You will need:

a sheet of red gift-wrap paper
a wand
invisible tape
an envelope large enough for your wand (you could make this from brown paper)

EFFECT

The magician taps a red wand on the table to show it is solid and then holds it in the air for the audience to see. The magician then holds up a long, empty envelope, puts the red wand into it, and casts a spell over it.

Pausing a moment for the spell to work, the magician opens the envelope and takes out a *black and white* wand — it has changed color!

The magician then crushes the envelope to show nothing remains inside it.

THE SECRET

The 'red' wand is simply a cylinder of red gift paper wrapped around the wand (it is known as a 'shell'). The 'shell' is left behind in the envelope when the wand is taken out and then crushed inside the envelope.

MAKING THE SECRET

You will need to prepare two items for this trick: the 'shell' and the envelope.

1
Get a sheet of red gift wrapping paper and cut it to fit closely but not tightly around the main length of your wand. Stick the edges with invisible tape as shown. This is the 'shell'.

2
To make the envelope, get some brown paper and make an envelope big enough to hold your wand.

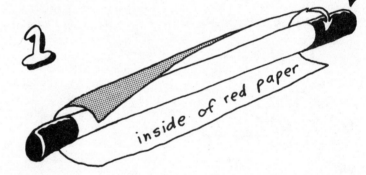

wand

inside of red paper

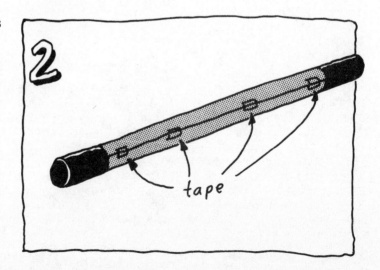

tape

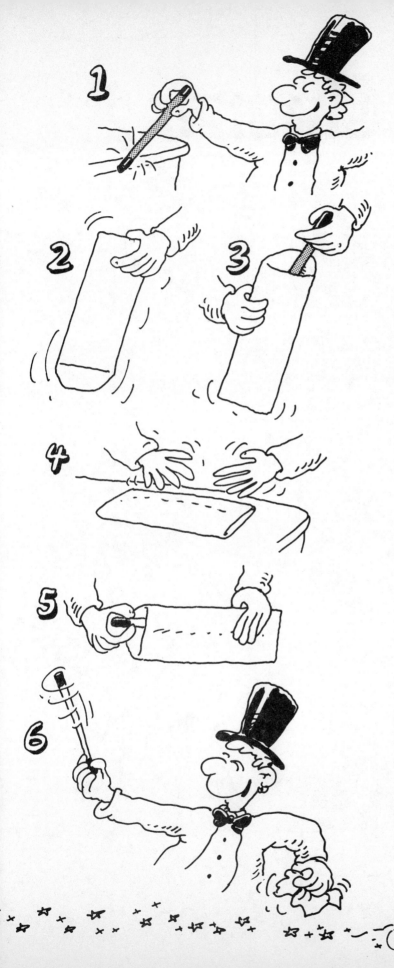

METHOD

1 'Ladies and gentlemen,' you announce, 'I'd like you to witness a simple demonstration of the magic powers of my red wand.'

Pick up the red wand and tap it on the table edge to show it is solid.

2 'Here I have a large empty envelope,' you continue. Hold the envelope upside down with its flap open.

'It is empty of everything and full of nothing,' you add, allowing the envelope to flop around to show it is empty.

3 'I will now place the red wand in the envelope and cast a magic spell over it.'

Put the red wand in the envelope, tuck in the opening flap and lie it on the table.

4 'Bim Salla Bim and Hocus Pocus,' you cry, gesturing with both hands towards the closed envelope.

5 Then you pick up the envelope with your left hand, open the flap with your right, and announce: 'Just as I thought.'

Squeezing the wand 'shell' through the envelope with the left hand, draw out the wand from inside the 'shell' with the right hand, 'Voila! The wand has changed color!'

6 Without drawing attention to it, you crush the envelope in your left hand to indicate that nothing solid remains in it.

'My wand has very special magic powers,' you say, taking a bow.

Paper Hoops

This trick never fails, provides good 'audience participation' and is fun for all.

You will need:
2 pair of scissors
glue
enough sheets of newspaper
  to make 3 strips each
  6" wide x 6 feet long.

EFFECT

1
The magician calls for two volunteers who stand on each side of the performer while their task is explained.

'I want you to watch closely,' the magician says, 'because soon I'll want you both to do what I'm about to demonstrate. There is a prize for the one who finishes first.'

The magician holds up a long hoop made of newspaper in the left hand and a pair of scissors in the right hand. 'Starting anywhere in the hoop, I'm going to cut along its length to form two separate hoops. Then I want you to do the same thing. The first one to finish cutting two hoops like this will be the winner.'

2
The magician cuts along the length of the hoop until two hoops have been cut. Putting the left arm through one hoop, it hangs from the magician's left shoulder; the magician then puts the right hand through the other hoop and hangs it from the right shoulder.

6

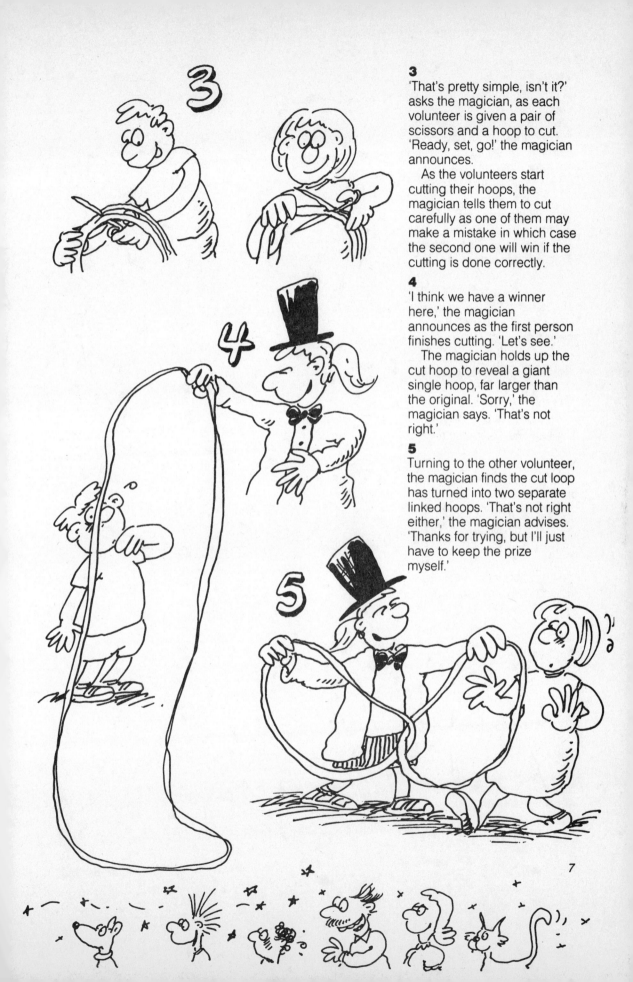

3

'That's pretty simple, isn't it?' asks the magician, as each volunteer is given a pair of scissors and a hoop to cut. 'Ready, set, go!' the magician announces.

As the volunteers start cutting their hoops, the magician tells them to cut carefully as one of them may make a mistake in which case the second one will win if the cutting is done correctly.

4

'I think we have a winner here,' the magician announces as the first person finishes cutting. 'Let's see.'

The magician holds up the cut hoop to reveal a giant single hoop, far larger than the original. 'Sorry,' the magician says. 'That's not right.'

5

Turning to the other volunteer, the magician finds the cut loop has turned into two separate linked hoops. 'That's not right either,' the magician advises. 'Thanks for trying, but I'll just have to keep the prize myself.'

THE SECRET

The three hoops are made by cutting and joining strips of newspaper to make one long strip about 6" wide and 6 feet long, and pasting the ends together. However, each one varies slightly.

1
The one the magician cuts as a demonstration has no special features. Make sure there are no twists in the paper when you join the ends.

2
The second has a *half twist* in its length before the ends are pasted together.

3
The third one has a *full twist* in its length before the ends are pasted together.

The twists are not seen by the audience because they are disguised in the long loops of newspaper.

When you prepare these hoops for a performance, make sure you do not crease them and *always* put the one you are going to use (the one without any twists) on top of the others. This way you'll know which one to use. The sequence of the other two doesn't matter.

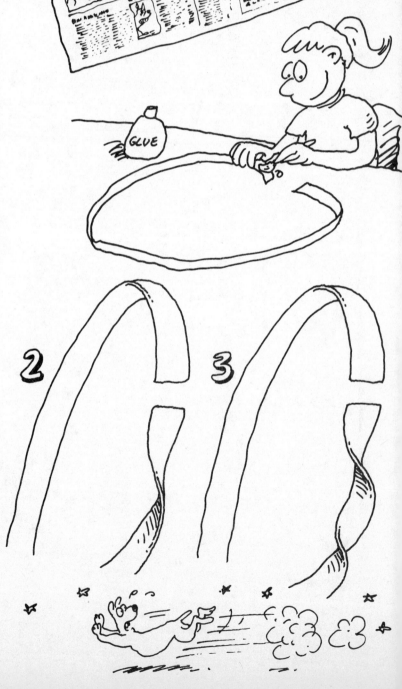

Follow the Leader

This trick is simpler to do than it first appears but it is quite mystifying.

You will need:

2 packs of playing cards

EFFECT

The magician selects a volunteer from the audience and explains that he must do everything that the magician, the 'Leader', does. They each shuffle a deck of cards, swap packs, shuffle them once more, then swap them back again. The magician and the volunteer then each select a card which must be remembered from the pack they are holding, place it on top of the deck and then cut the cards to bury the selected one in the pack. The packs are exchanged again and the magician now says that the duplicate of the chosen card is to be removed from the pack each person now has. Both cards are turned up and they are identical!

METHOD

1

Give one card deck to a volunteer, keeping the other one yourself. Explain to the volunteer that you are the 'leader' and that he must follow every move you make, using the pack you've just given him.

2

Shuffle your deck thoroughly and make sure the volunteer does the same with his. Exchange decks and both of you shuffle them again.

3

Make this shuffle quite theatrical and remind the audience that the volunteer must 'follow the leader'. When the volunteer tries to copy your shuffle, the audience's attention will be drawn to him. While the audience is diverted, you secretly sneak a look at the bottom card of the deck you are holding and remember it.

4

Exchange decks again. Then say this to the volunteer: 'Remove a card from the deck you are holding, any card, and remember it. I will do the same.'

You select a card as well, but *make no effort to remember it*. (It is important to remember the one you saw on the bottom of the volunteer's deck previously.)

5

Tell the volunteer to put his selected card face down on top of his pack, as you do the same with your pack.

6

'Now we both cut our decks once and put the bottom pile on top of the selected card, thus burying it in the deck.' You both do this.

7

Exchange card decks once again. Say to the volunteer: 'I want you to go through my deck, which you are now holding, and remove the duplicate of the card you selected and put it face down on top. I will do the same with your deck.'

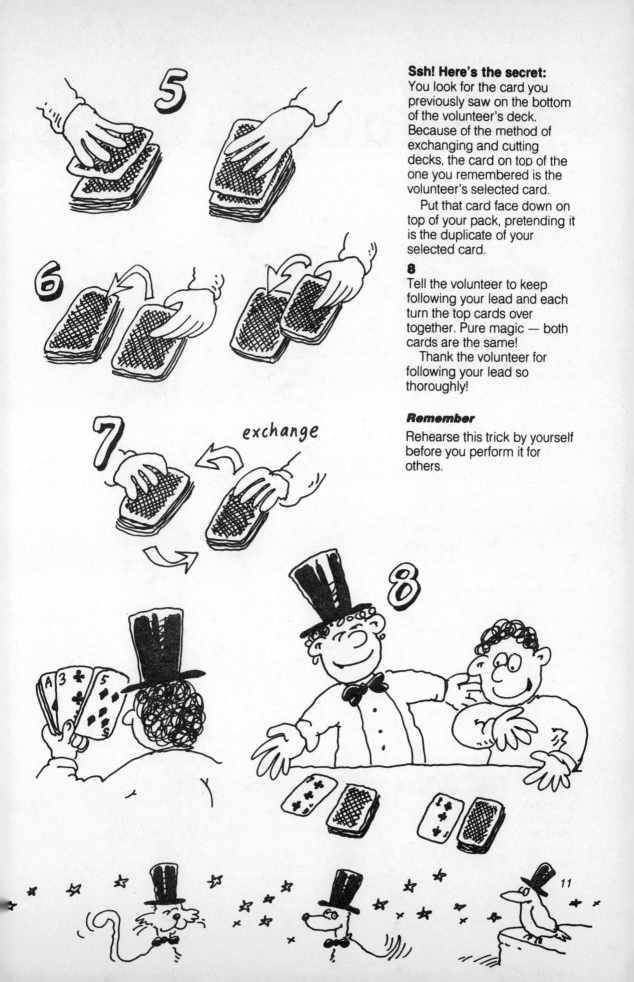

5

6

7

exchange

8

Ssh! Here's the secret:
You look for the card you previously saw on the bottom of the volunteer's deck. Because of the method of exchanging and cutting decks, the card on top of the one you remembered is the volunteer's selected card.

Put that card face down on top of your pack, pretending it is the duplicate of your selected card.

8
Tell the volunteer to keep following your lead and each turn the top cards over together. Pure magic — both cards are the same!

Thank the volunteer for following your lead so thoroughly!

Remember
Rehearse this trick by yourself before you perform it for others.

Coin through Glass

A little practice and you'll amaze everyone with this simple trick.

You will need:

a coin
a large handkerchief
a drinking glass
a left-hand pocket
a rubber band (kept in your
  left pocket)
a wand

EFFECT

The magician puts a coin under a handkerchief and drops it into a glass. A rubber band is placed around the rim of the glass over the handkerchief to keep the coin inside.

   The handkerchief-covered glass is given to a spectator to hold while the magician makes several passes over it with his wand and casts a magic charm. The spectator removes the handkerchief and the coin has completely vanished!

METHOD

1
Show the coin between your right thumb and forefinger.

2
Produce the handkerchief and drape it over the coin. Change your grip so that you are holding the coin through the handkerchief in your right hand.

3

Take the glass in your left hand and hold it behind the handkerchief and below the coin, saying: 'I will now drop the coin into the glass.'

4

Now to the secret move: Tilt the angle of the glass in your left hand (it's behind the hanky and won't be noticed) so that the dropped coin clinks as it strikes the outside of the glass and drops into your left palm. The audience will think the coin is inside the glass.

5

Put down the glass (covered with the handkerchief) with your right hand. At the same time put your left hand in your pocket, leave the coin there, and bring out the rubber band.

6

Use the rubber band to secure the handkerchief to the rim of the glass. Hand the glass to a member of the audience — do not allow any shaking of the glass or looking under the handkerchief. Wave your wand over the glass several times and, after giving your magic chant, invite the audience member to remove the rubber band and handkerchief. Hey, presto! The coin has vanished!

Remember

Practice every step of this trick thoroughly. Make certain the clinking of the falling coin on the outside of the glass can be heard. Do not repeat this trick to the same audience.

Money to Burn

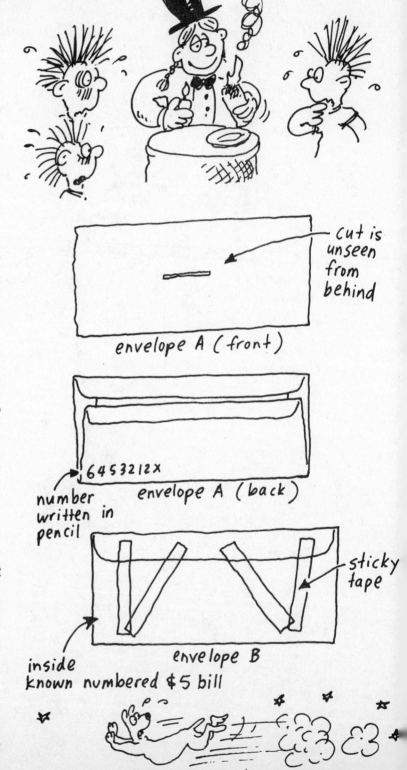

This simple, effective trick really involves your audience and keeps them guessing!

You will need:

2 small envelopes
1 five-dollar bill
sticky tape
a saucer
a notepad and pen
a cigarette lighter
a pocket somewhere in your clothes.

EFFECT

The magican calls for three audience members to assist with the next trick. One is presented with a sealed and taped envelope to hold, another is appointed 'Secretary' and given the notepad and pen, and the third is asked for a five-dollar bill.

The magician goes back to the stage, reads out the number on the five-dollar bill for the 'Secretary' to record, and places the money in an envelope and seals it.

The magician brings the cigarette lighter from her pocket and holding the sealed envelope containing the money over the saucer, sets it alight. Commenting that the donor has 'money to burn', the magician offers him the charred envelope on the saucer.

The magician then asks the first volunteer to open the sealed envelope. This

cut is unseen from behind

envelope A (front)

6453212x

number written in pencil

envelope A (back)

sticky tape

inside known numbered $5 bill

envelope B

volunteer finds a five-dollar bill inside and is amazed after checking with the 'Secretary' that it has the original number on it!

THE SECRET

Both envelopes are specially prepared beforehand. Envelope A, into which the five-dollar bill is placed, has a 2" slit cut in its face which cannot be seen from the back of the envelope when it is opened. On the lower left corner of the back of this envelope (A) you also write, in pencil, the number of a *different* five-dollar bill.

Envelope B, which you give to the first volunteer at the start, has this different five-dollar note inside it. This envelope (B) is sealed and crossed with sticky tape (to make it difficult to open).

METHOD

1
Hand out the sealed envelope (B) and the notepad and pen to two different volunteers.

2
Ask for the loan of a five-dollar bill from the audience. (The loaned note must be the same value as the one already hidden in envelope B.) Fold the borrowed note three times and place it in envelope A.

3
Then, as if you've forgotten to read out the note's number, take the note out and unfold it, asking the 'Secretary' to write down the number you read out. Of course the number you read out is the one you wrote in pencil on the back of the envelope.

4

Then fold the note again and appear to enclose it in the envelope while actually passing it through the slit into your left hand. Seal the envelope and take it in your right hand, leaving the note hidden in your left hand.

5

Put your left hand in your pocket, leaving the five-dollar bill there, and produce the cigarette lighter.

6

Set a corner of envelope A on fire and allow it to burn freely in the saucer. Then confess your 'failure' and offer the charred paper to the donor remarking that he has 'money to burn'. Allow the donor to worry for a moment about the apparent loss of his money, then ask the first volunteer to open his envelope in which the five dollars is discovered. Its number is the same as the one read out earlier. Amazing!

Remember

Learn all these moves thoroughly and you will astound your audience. Only perform this trick when you can be no less than 6 feet from your audience and do not repeat it to the same group.

Predicting the Stars

The extravagant way you present this simple trick adds to the mystery it creates...

You will need:

a notepad, 7.5" x 5"
  with ten to twelve pages (or
  an equal number of sheets
  of paper)
a plastic bowl
a large envelope
a bold marker pen
an 8½" x 11" sheet of paper

EFFECT

1
The magician asks the audience to call out the names of their favorite television stars.

2
The magician writes each on a separate piece of notepaper, folds it several times and places it in the bowl, mixing it with the others.

3
The magician makes a prediction about which of these names will be drawn from the bowl and writes it, unseen, on the sheet of 8½" x 11" paper, folds it and seals it in the envelope which is given to a spectator to hold.

4

Another member of the audience is asked to draw one name from the bowl and announce it to the others.

5

The spectator with the envelope is then asked to open it and reveal the magician's prediction. Amazingly, the magician has chosen the very same name!

Madonna!

THE SECRET

As the names of the television stars are called out, the magician, unseen by the audience, simply writes the first called name over and over again so that each slip has exactly the same name on it. The magician's prediction is, of course, that name. Success is guaranteed!

METHOD

It is important that the audience believe each slip of paper has a different name on it, so do the writing above their line of sight — by having them sit on the floor, for example.

Play with the audience a little by asking them how to spell some of the names called. This will convince them you are writing each one down.

Fold each slip several times so the names cannot be seen.

When asking a member of the audience to draw a name from the bowl, hold the bowl overhead so the contents cannot be seen. While that name (the first one called) is being shown to the audience, quickly dispose of the other slips so you can't be found out!

Then ask for your prediction to be removed from its envelope and announced.

Isn't it simple?

Disappearing Dice

Now you see it, now you don't! This dramatic trick, which you can make yourself, will fool, confuse and surprise your audience.

You will need:

a large hat
a wand
a ruler
a pencil
an eraser
scissors or a Stanley knife
glue
thin black cardboard 20.5" x 31.5"
42 white adhesive spots (you can get these from a stationer)

EFFECT

The magician puts a hat on the table in front of the audience and places a large dice on top of it. A dice cover is placed over the dice and, after a wave of the magic wand, the cover is removed to reveal that the dice has disappeared.

The dice is found *inside* the hat, having passed through it. The magician then hands the dice and the hat to the audience for inspection.

THE SECRET

A special dice 'shell' which has no base and fits neatly over the real dice is used.

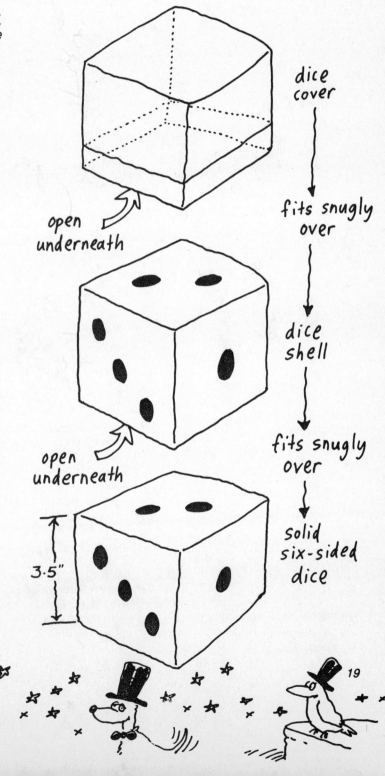

dice cover

open underneath

fits snugly over

dice shell

open underneath

fits snugly over

3.5"

solid six-sided dice

MAKING THE SECRET

Take your time making this equipment. The neater and more accurately you do it, the better it will work and the longer it will last.

Solid Dice

1
Draw this plan to the correct size (i.e. double the size shown here) on your sheet of cardboard.

2
In pencil write the numbers shown here on your plan.

3
Cut out the shape with a Stanley knife, then fold where indicated and see your dice emerge.

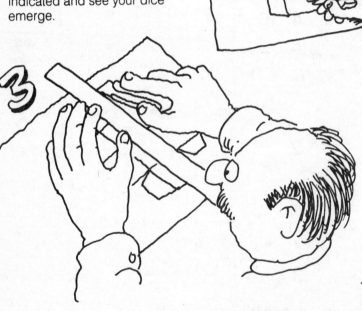

4
The flaps go on the inside and should be glued two at a time only. Wait until the glue dries before fixing the next two, etc. This will help you get a good, balanced shape and lets you adjust any side that fits poorly.

20

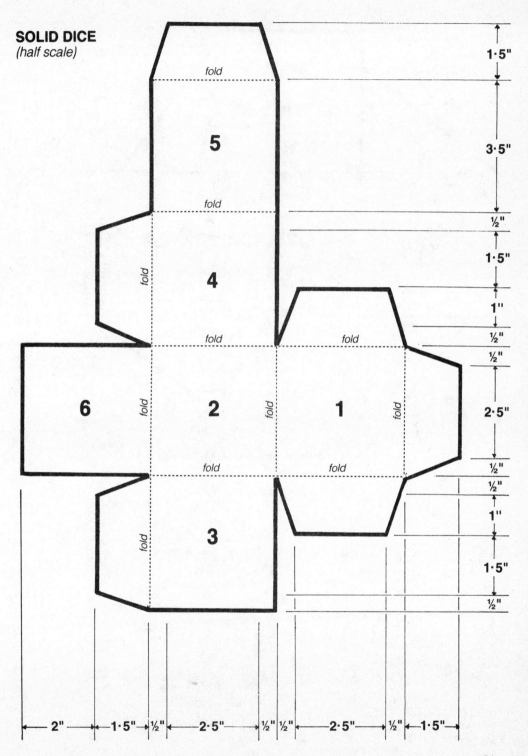

SOLID DICE
(half scale)

5

fold

4

fold

6

2

1

3

fold

1·5"

3·5"

½"

1·5"

1"

½"

½"

2·5"

½"

½"

1"

1·5"

½"

2" 1·5" ½" 2·5" ½" ½" 2·5" ½" 1·5"

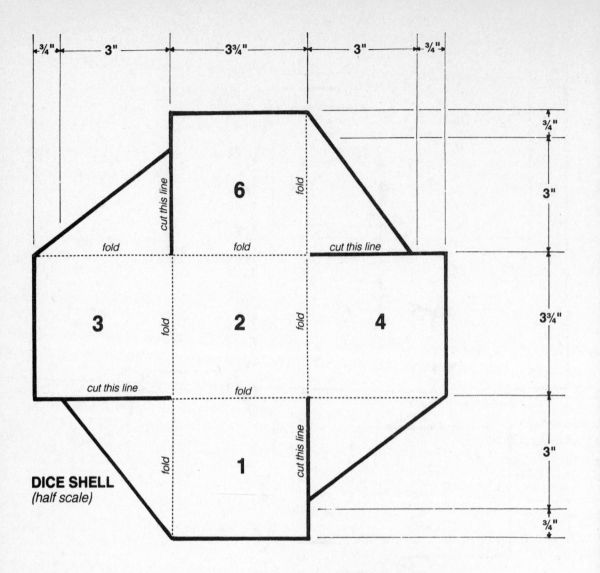

¾" | 3" | 3¾" | 3" | ¾"

¾"

3"

3¾"

3"

¾"

6

fold

cut this line

fold

cut this line

fold

3

fold

2

fold

4

cut this line

fold

fold

1

cut this line

DICE SHELL
(half scale)

Dice Shell

Draw this plan to the correct size (i.e. double the size shown here) on your cardboard.

Pencil-in the numbers shown.

Cut out the shape and fold along the lines indicated.

Glue the flaps inside the box.

When finished, the Dice Shell should fit snuggly over the Solid Dice just completed.

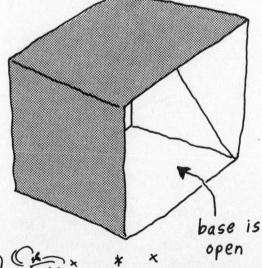

base is open

22

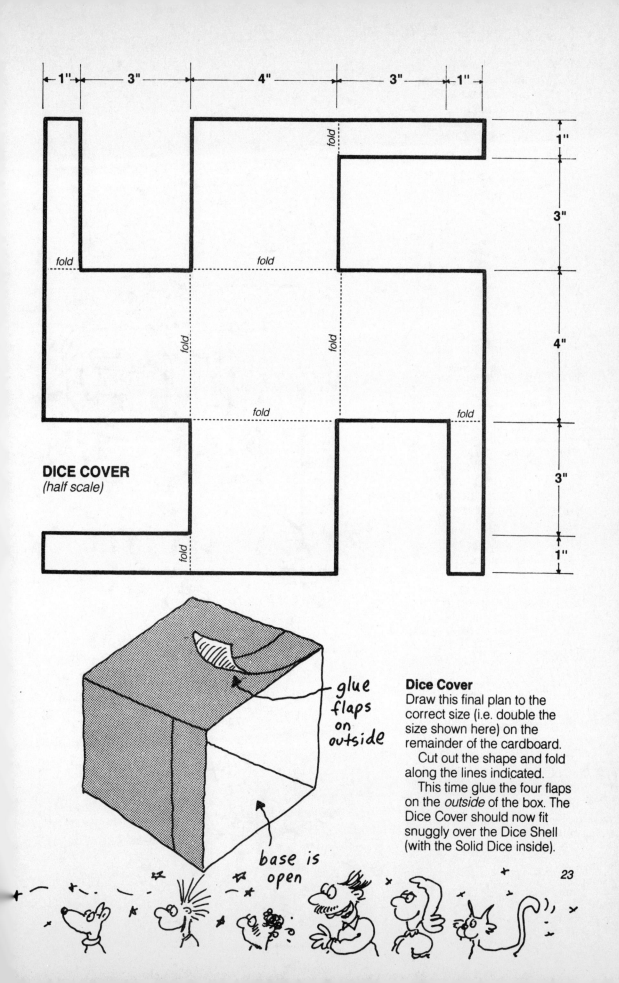

←1"→ ←——3"——→ ←———————4"———————→ ←———3"———→ ←—1"—→

fold

1"

3"

fold   fold

fold   fold

4"

DICE COVER
(half scale)

fold   fold

3"

fold

1"

glue
flaps
on
outside

base is
open

Dice Cover
Draw this final plan to the
correct size (i.e. double the
size shown here) on the
remainder of the cardboard.

Cut out the shape and fold
along the lines indicated.

This time glue the four flaps
on the *outside* of the box. The
Dice Cover should now fit
snuggly over the Dice Shell
(with the Solid Dice inside).

23

Decorating the equipment

The Solid Dice and the Dice Shell have to appear identical. To do this it is necessary to put dots on them both. (Remember that the dots on opposite sides of dice always add up to seven.) You can buy adhesive dots from your stationer and use these.

The Dice Cover can be painted with symbols or the outside can be re-covered in wallpaper.

METHOD

1

Before you begin this trick, hide the Solid Dice inside the Dice Shell. Make sure the position of the spots on the Dice Shell matches exactly the position of the spots on the Solid Dice. Practice holding the Solid Dice inside the Dice Shell with simple finger and thumb pressure on the sides. You are now ready to perform the trick.

2

With a flourish you produce a hat and an oversized dice saying: 'Ladies and gentlemen, today, right before your eyes, I am going to make this dice disappear.' The Solid Dice is hidden inside the Dice Shell.

3

'I will start by placing the dice on top of the hat and I will make it pass right through the hat and reappear inside it.' So saying, you tilt the hat towards the audience pretending to demonstrate the passage of the dice through the hat.

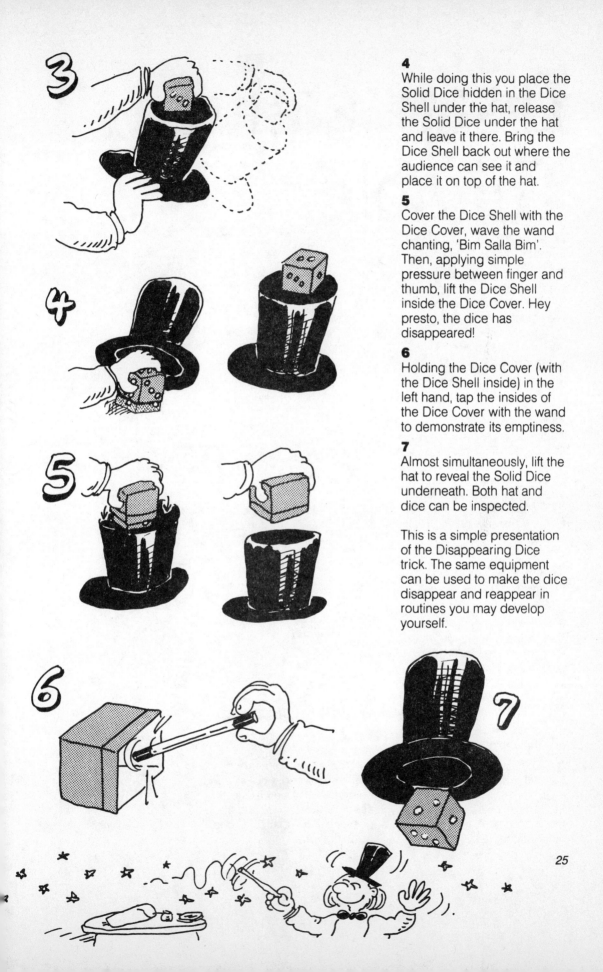

4
While doing this you place the Solid Dice hidden in the Dice Shell under the hat, release the Solid Dice under the hat and leave it there. Bring the Dice Shell back out where the audience can see it and place it on top of the hat.

5
Cover the Dice Shell with the Dice Cover, wave the wand chanting, 'Bim Salla Bim'. Then, applying simple pressure between finger and thumb, lift the Dice Shell inside the Dice Cover. Hey presto, the dice has disappeared!

6
Holding the Dice Cover (with the Dice Shell inside) in the left hand, tap the insides of the Dice Cover with the wand to demonstrate its emptiness.

7
Almost simultaneously, lift the hat to reveal the Solid Dice underneath. Both hat and dice can be inspected.

This is a simple presentation of the Disappearing Dice trick. The same equipment can be used to make the dice disappear and reappear in routines you may develop yourself.

Disappearing Thimble

Because they are light and small, thimbles are one of the easiest objects for 'beginner' magicians to manipulate.

You will need:

1 loosely fitting plastic thimble

EFFECT

A thimble is placed on the magician's right forefinger and held up to the audience. The magician removes it with the clenched left hand and it totally disappears — only to be found later in an unexpected place.

THE SECRET

Professional magicians call this a 'Thumb Palm'.

1

Put the thimble on your right forefinger. Have your palm facing downwards; clench your other three fingers.

2

Quickly bend your finger so the thimble is between your palm and the ball of your thumb.

3

Close the base of your thumb so that it grips the thimble. At the same time, straighten your forefinger again, leaving the hidden thimble behind.

Practice this movement until you can do it quickly and confidently. Then practice it some more to eliminate all possibility of fumbles, drops or hesitations.

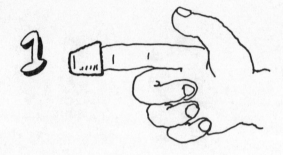

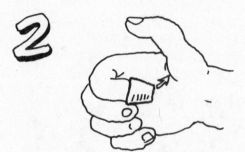

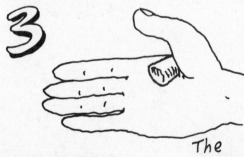

The Thumb Palm

METHOD

When you have perfected the 'Thumb Palm', you are ready to begin the Disappearing Thimble trick.

1
Place the thimble on your right forefinger and turn the back of your hand towards the audience holding it at shoulder height.

2
Move your right, up-pointed hand fully across your body to the left, transferring your weight to your left foot and twisting your body so that your right shoulder is towards the audience. The back of your hand is still towards your audience.

3
At the same time bring your clenched left hand just above your bent right elbow, and, in a sweeping movement, raise your left hand up your arm, over the back of your pointed right hand as if pulling the thimble off your fingertip.

4

At the precise moment your moving left hand shields the thimble from the audience, quickly 'Thumb Palm' the thimble and straighten your right forefinger again; i.e. the thimble never leaves your right hand. Keep your clenched left hand, knuckles towards the audience, just above your pointing right finger.

5

Your audience will see the thimble is not on your right forefinger and assume, as you want them to, that it's in the palm of your left hand. To encourage that thought, keep pointing with your right forefinger at your clenched left hand and start moving your clenched left fingers as if squeezing the imaginary thimble to pulp.

6

Continue 'squeezing' and gradually lower your right hand, while gazing at your left hand to help misdirect your audience. Then slowly turn your left palm to the audience and open your fingers to reveal an empty hand. Hey presto — the thimble has disappeared.

7

As you look around in amazement to find the lost thimble, quietly slip your right forefinger back into the palmed thimble (don't let the audience see you do this).

Pretend to look for the missing thimble behind your left knee, bending slightly and using your extended left forefinger to search. 'No, not there,' you say.

Then, straightening up, bend slightly to the right as you put your right hand

4

R / L

right hand hidden during thumb palm

L

L

thimble's gone! It seems to be in left hand but is palmed in right

R

5

6

7

behind your right knee and announce 'Here it is!' Bring your right hand up with the thimble on your extended forefinger for the audience to see.

Remember

Patter is not important during this trick; but use the suggested words at the very end.

Practice the body movements and sequence carefully.

Do not repeat this trick to the same audience; simply move on to the following thimble trick.

Swinging Thimble Dance

This is an ideal follow-up trick to the Disappearing Thimble, but first you must perfect Thumb Palming with your left hand as well as your right. When you are comfortable doing it in both hands, you are ready for this highly entertaining trick.

You will need:

2 identical, loosely fitting thimbles
1 chair (optional)

EFFECT

Standing on one foot, the magician raises the right knee and places the hands on either side of the knee. The backs of the magician's hands face the audience and there is a thimble on the right forefinger. The magician commences a pendulum motion by moving the right hand in an arc about 20" to the right of the raised knee and letting it swing back to the knee. The magician then continues the pendulum motion with the left hand, moving it a similar distance from the knee. As the magician continues this swaying motion with both hands, the thimble appears to leap from the right forefinger to the left forefinger and back again!

THE SECRET

You guessed it — start with a Thumb Palmed thimble in your left hand and simply alternate palming a thimble in each hand.

METHOD

1

Stand on your left foot with your right knee raised. If you find this difficult, rest the toe of your right foot on a chair placed beside and slightly behind you. Have a thimble on your extended right hand and a palmed thimble in your left hand.

2

Place your left and right hands on either side of your raised knee.

3

Swing your right hand about 20" to the right of your knee (leaving your left hand, with palmed thimble, against your knee).

4

Swing the right hand back to its original position beside your knee, palming the thimble as you do so.

5

As the right hand (with thimble hidden) reaches the knee, continue the pendulum motion by swinging your left hand, now with thimble exposed, about 20" to the left of your knee.

Then retrace that arc by letting the left hand swing back to your knee, palming the thimble again as it arrives.

Repeat this procedure three or four times. The thimble appears to jump over your knee onto the other hand — that's why it's called the Swinging Thimble Dance!

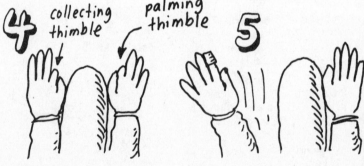

unseen palmed thimble

raised right knee (as the magician sees it)

20 inches

collecting thimble

palming thimble

Finish the trick by bowing to your audience and putting one hand in your pocket to unload one palmed thimble.

Remember

Do not rush the presentation of this trick — develop a casual pendulum swing that appears continuous.

It is best not to speak while you are performing. Let your practiced fingers do the talking!

Magic Rope

A wonderful trick which will convince your audience that you really do have magic powers — there's just no other explanation!

You will need:

1 x 9 feet 9" length of rope
2 x 15" lengths of rope
a watch or a rubber band
a jacket with an inside pocket
NOTE: Stage magicians prefer a white, flexible cord of about ⅓" diameter as it is easy for the audience to see, it doesn't unravel, and it is easy to handle. Try to find some.

EFFECT

The magician displays two short pieces of rope, ties two ends of one piece together to form a loop, passes the second short piece through the loop and ties its ends together, so that the pieces are linked. Swaying the linked loops together, the magician blows on them and they mysteriously separate.

The magician then appears to stretch one piece of rope until its length is increased tenfold!

THE SECRET

The long piece of rope is carefully coiled in the magician's inside jacket pocket. One end is pulled down the inside of the sleeve and secured under the watchband (or a rubber band) at the wrist.

rope concealed inside sleeve

METHOD

1

Show the two short pieces of rope to the audience and tie one into a loop.

2

Place one end of the second short piece through the loop and appear to tie the second short piece into another loop. Hook the first loop with your right little finger to leave your right thumb and forefinger free to tie the next knot. What you really do is hold one end in your *left* hand with your little finger and ring finger and tie the other to the end of the rope that was under your watchband.

3

The audience thinks the two short ropes have been linked. Hold the loops together, swaying them backwards and forwards and blow for effect on where they appear to cross. During this swaying movement bring the first loop (held in the right hand) around the bottom of the left loop and up under the end held against your left palm by your little and ring fingers, momentarily relaxing your grip to allow it to pass underneath the untied end. You will need to turn the loop held in your right hand during this manoeuvre. Practice this carefully. Show the separated loop to the audience.

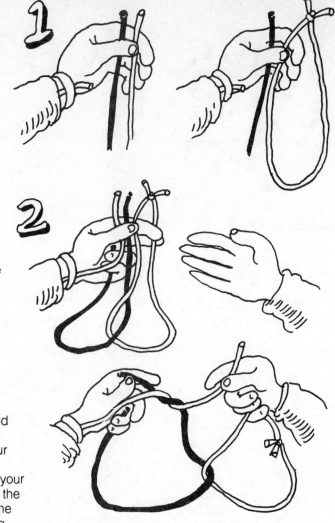

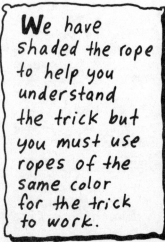

We have shaded the rope to help you understand the trick but you must use ropes of the same color for the trick to work.